# The BIG eBook Upload & Update Log

## Indie Book Management

Book # _____

From: _____ to _____

**WestWard Journals**

WestWard Books

Payson, Arizona

WestWard Journals

Cover Photo by Lukas Blazek on Unsplash

ISBN-13: 978-1-947306-15-8

# INTRODUCTION

This Log contains space to make note of upload and update details for twenty self-published ebooks. The book is designed to be used with Kindle Direct Publishing. It contains ample pages for notes about updates and changes, which should help keep track of any details the Indie or Self-Publishing Author and Publisher may need.

# MY PROJECT IDEAS

# MY BOOKS

Book 1    Title _____    Page 1

_____

Book 2    Title _____    Page 9

_____

Book 3    Title _____    Page 17

_____

Book 4    Title _____    Page 25

_____

Book 5    Title _____    Page 33

_____

Book 6    Title _____    Page 41

_____

Book 7    Title _____    Page 49

_____

Book 8    Title _____    Page 57

_____

Book 9    Title _____    Page 65

_____

Book 10   Title _____    Page 73

_____

# BOOK 1 - Date _____

## Kindle eBook Details

Language _____

Book Title _____

Subtitle _____

Series _____ # _____

Edition Number (optional) _____

Author _____

Contributors (opt) _____

_____

_____

_____

Description: _____

_____

_____

_____

_____

_____

_____

_____

_____

_____

_____

_____

_____

Publishing Rights (circle or underline one)

       I own the copyright

       This is a public domain work

**Book Title** _____

Keywords (seven words or phrases)

_____

_____

_____

_____

_____

_____

_____

Categories (two)

_____

_____

_____

_____

Age & Grade Range

Children's Book age range (optional)

     Minimum _____          Maximum _____

U.S. grade range

     Minimum _____          Maximum _____

Adult Content         No     Yes

## Kindle eBook Content

Manuscript

    Digital Rights Management (DRM)

    Enable DRM on this Kindle eBooks?

        Yes _____      No _____

**Book Title** _____

Recommended formats for Kindle eBooks:
.doc, .docx, HTML, MOBI, ePub, RTF, Plain Text, and KPF.

Upload eBook manuscript
File name _____
Uploaded          Date _____
Spell Check
      ("Ignore All" doesn't always work)

File Updated       Date _____
File Updated       Date _____
File Updated       Date _____
**Interior Formatter** _____
Contact Info: _____
Cost: _____

Kindle eBook Cover (check one)
    ___ Use Cover Creator to make your book cover
    ___ Upload a cover you already have (JPG/TIFF only)

Upload your cover file
File name _____
Uploaded          Date _____
Kindle eBook Preview via Online Previewer
    ___ Launch Previewer       Approved date: _____
Downloadable Preview Options
      ___ On your computer        ___ On your Kindle device

**Book Title** _____

      Cover Updated    Date _____

      Cover Updated    Date _____

      Cover Updated    Date _____

      **Cover Designer** _____

      Contact Info: _____

      Cost: _____

ISBN (Optional Choice)

      Kindle ISBN _____

      Your ISBN _____

      Publisher (optional) _____

## Kindle eBook Pricing

KDP Select Enrollment (Optional)    Yes ____      No ____

Territories (check one)

      ____ All territories

      ____ Individual territories (Note all your choices below)

_____

_____

_____

_____

_____

_____

_____

_____

_____

**Book Title** _____

Royalty & Pricing - Select a royalty plan and set your Kindle eBook list prices below.

   ___ 30%      ___ 70%

Your book file size after conversion is _____

Primary Marketplace _____

List Price Chosen _____   Currency _____

Rate _____   Delivery _____   Royalty _____

* Other Marketplace _____

List Price Chosen _____   Currency _____

Rate _____   Delivery _____   Royalty _____

* Other Marketplace _____

List Price Chosen _____   Currency _____

Rate _____   Delivery _____   Royalty _____

* Other Marketplace _____

List Price Chosen _____   Currency _____

Rate _____   Delivery _____   Royalty _____

* Other Marketplace _____

List Price Chosen _____   Currency _____

Rate _____   Delivery _____   Royalty _____

* Other Marketplace _____

List Price Chosen _____   Currency _____

Rate _____   Delivery _____   Royalty _____

**Book Title** _____

\* Other Marketplace _____

List Price Chosen _____ Currency _____

Rate _____ Delivery _____ Royalty _____

\* Other Marketplace _____

List Price Chosen _____ Currency _____

Rate _____ Delivery _____ Royalty _____

\* Other Marketplace _____

List Price Chosen _____ Currency _____

Rate _____ Delivery _____ Royalty _____

\* Other Marketplace _____

List Price Chosen _____ Currency _____

Rate _____ Delivery _____ Royalty _____

\* Other Marketplace _____

List Price Chosen _____ Currency _____

Rate _____ Delivery _____ Royalty _____

\* Other Marketplace _____

List Price Chosen _____ Currency _____

Rate _____ Delivery _____ Royalty _____

\* Other Marketplace _____

List Price Chosen _____ Currency _____

Rate _____ Delivery _____ Royalty _____

**Book Title** _____

Matchbook

___ Enroll my book in Kindle Matchbook

Book Lending

___ Allow Kindle Book Lending

Terms & Conditions ___ Read

Save as Draft Date _____

Clicked Publish Your Kindle eBook Date _____

Published Notice from KDP Date _____

## Note Date & Changes Made

_____

_____

_____

_____

_____

_____

_____

_____

_____

_____

_____

_____

_____

_____

_____

_____

_____

**Book Title** _____

## Note Date & Changes Made

_____

_____

_____

_____

_____

_____

_____

_____

_____

_____

_____

_____

_____

_____

_____

_____

_____

_____

_____

_____

_____

_____

_____

_____

_____

# BOOK 2 - Date _____

## Kindle eBook Details

Language _____

Book Title _____

Subtitle _____

Series _____ # _____

Edition Number (optional) _____

Author _____

Contributors (opt) _____

_____

_____

_____

Description: _____

_____

_____

_____

_____

_____

_____

_____

_____

_____

_____

_____

Publishing Rights (circle or underline one)

      I own the copyright

      This is a public domain work

**Book Title** _____

Keywords (seven words or phrases)

_____

_____

_____

_____

_____

_____

_____

Categories (two)

_____

_____

_____

_____

Age & Grade Range

Children's Book age range (optional)

    Minimum _____         Maximum _____

U.S. grade range

    Minimum _____         Maximum _____

Adult Content          No     Yes

## Kindle eBook Content

Manuscript

    Digital Rights Management (DRM)

    Enable DRM on this Kindle eBooks?

        Yes _____       No _____

**Book Title** _____

Recommended formats for Kindle eBooks:

.doc, .docx, HTML, MOBI, ePub, RTF, Plain Text, and KPF.

Upload eBook manuscript

File name _____

Uploaded      Date _____

Spell Check

     ("Ignore All" doesn't always work)

File Updated      Date _____

File Updated      Date _____

File Updated      Date _____

**Interior Formatter** _____

Contact Info: _____

Cost: _____

Kindle eBook Cover (check one)

     ___ Use Cover Creator to make your book cover

     ___ Upload a cover you already have (JPG/TIFF only)

Upload your cover file

File name _____

Uploaded      Date _____

Kindle eBook Preview via Online Previewer

     ___ Launch Previewer      Approved date: _____

Downloadable Preview Options

     ___ On your computer      ___ On your Kindle device

**Book Title** _____

    Cover Updated   Date _____

    Cover Updated   Date _____

    Cover Updated   Date _____

    **Cover Designer** _____

    Contact Info: _____

    Cost: _____

ISBN (Optional Choice)

    Kindle ISBN _____

    Your ISBN _____

    Publisher (optional) _____

**Kindle eBook Pricing**

KDP Select Enrollment (Optional)   Yes ____    No ____

Territories (check one)

    ____ All territories

    ____ Individual territories (Note all your choices below)

_____

_____

_____

_____

_____

_____

_____

_____

**Book Title** _____

Royalty & Pricing - Select a royalty plan and set your Kindle eBook list prices below.

_____ 30%          _____ 70%

Your book file size after conversion is _____

Primary Marketplace _____

List Price Chosen _____     Currency _____

Rate _____   Delivery _____   Royalty _____


* Other Marketplace _____

List Price Chosen _____     Currency _____

Rate _____   Delivery _____   Royalty _____


* Other Marketplace _____

List Price Chosen _____     Currency _____

Rate _____   Delivery _____   Royalty _____


* Other Marketplace _____

List Price Chosen _____     Currency _____

Rate _____   Delivery _____   Royalty _____


* Other Marketplace _____

List Price Chosen _____     Currency _____

Rate _____   Delivery _____   Royalty _____


* Other Marketplace _____

List Price Chosen _____     Currency _____

Rate _____   Delivery _____   Royalty _____

**Book Title** _____

* Other Marketplace _____

List Price Chosen _____        Currency _____

Rate _____        Delivery _____        Royalty _____


* Other Marketplace _____

List Price Chosen _____        Currency _____

Rate _____        Delivery _____        Royalty _____


* Other Marketplace _____

List Price Chosen _____        Currency _____

Rate _____        Delivery _____        Royalty _____


* Other Marketplace _____

List Price Chosen _____        Currency _____

Rate _____        Delivery _____        Royalty _____


* Other Marketplace _____

List Price Chosen _____        Currency _____

Rate _____        Delivery _____        Royalty _____


* Other Marketplace _____

List Price Chosen _____        Currency _____

Rate _____        Delivery _____        Royalty _____


* Other Marketplace _____

List Price Chosen _____        Currency _____

Rate _____        Delivery _____        Royalty _____

**Book Title** _____

Matchbook

___ Enroll my book in Kindle Matchbook

Book Lending

___ Allow Kindle Book Lending

Terms & Conditions ___ Read

Save as Draft Date _____

Clicked Publish Your Kindle eBook Date _____

Published Notice from KDP Date _____

## Note Date & Changes Made

_____

_____

_____

_____

_____

_____

_____

_____

_____

_____

_____

_____

_____

_____

_____

_____

_____

_____

_____

**Book Title** _____

## Note Date & Changes Made

_____

_____

_____

_____

_____

_____

_____

_____

_____

_____

_____

_____

_____

_____

_____

_____

_____

_____

_____

_____

_____

_____

# BOOK 3 - Date _____

## Kindle eBook Details

Language _____

Book Title _____

Subtitle _____

Series _____ # ____

Edition Number (optional) _____

Author _____

Contributors (opt) _____

_____

_____

_____

Description: _____

_____

_____

_____

_____

_____

_____

_____

_____

_____

_____

_____

Publishing Rights (circle or underline one)

      I own the copyright

      This is a public domain work

**Book Title** _____

Keywords (seven words or phrases)

_____

_____

_____

_____

_____

_____

_____

Categories (two)

_____

_____

_____

_____

Age & Grade Range

Children's Book age range (optional)

    Minimum _____        Maximum _____

U.S. grade range

    Minimum _____        Maximum _____

Adult Content         No    Yes

## Kindle eBook Content

Manuscript

    Digital Rights Management (DRM)

    Enable DRM on this Kindle eBooks?

        Yes _____      No _____

**Book Title** _____

Recommended formats for Kindle eBooks:
.doc, .docx, HTML, MOBI, ePub, RTF, Plain Text, and KPF.

Upload eBook manuscript
File name _____
Uploaded        Date _____
Spell Check
    ("Ignore All" doesn't always work)

File Updated        Date _____
File Updated        Date _____
File Updated        Date _____
**Interior Formatter** _____
Contact Info: _____
Cost: _____

Kindle eBook Cover (check one)
    ___ Use Cover Creator to make your book cover
    ___ Upload a cover you already have (JPG/TIFF only)

Upload your cover file
File name _____
Uploaded        Date _____
Kindle eBook Preview via Online Previewer
    ___ Launch Previewer        Approved date: _____
Downloadable Preview Options
    ___ On your computer        ___ On your Kindle device

**Book Title** _____

     Cover Updated   Date _____

     Cover Updated   Date _____

     Cover Updated   Date _____

     **Cover Designer** _____

     Contact Info: _____

     Cost: _____

ISBN (Optional Choice)

     Kindle ISBN _____

     Your ISBN _____

     Publisher (optional) _____

## Kindle eBook Pricing

KDP Select Enrollment (Optional)   Yes ___     No ___

Territories (check one)

     ___ All territories

     ___ Individual territories (Note all your choices below)

_____

_____

_____

_____

_____

_____

_____

_____

**Book Title** _____

Royalty & Pricing - Select a royalty plan and set your Kindle eBook list prices below.

___ 30%          ___ 70%

Your book file size after conversion is _____

Primary Marketplace _____

List Price Chosen _____     Currency _____

Rate _____     Delivery _____     Royalty _____


* Other Marketplace _____

List Price Chosen _____     Currency _____

Rate _____     Delivery _____     Royalty _____


* Other Marketplace _____

List Price Chosen _____     Currency _____

Rate _____     Delivery _____     Royalty _____


* Other Marketplace _____

List Price Chosen _____     Currency _____

Rate _____     Delivery _____     Royalty _____


* Other Marketplace _____

List Price Chosen _____     Currency _____

Rate _____     Delivery _____     Royalty _____


* Other Marketplace _____

List Price Chosen _____     Currency _____

Rate _____     Delivery _____     Royalty _____

**Book Title** _____

&ast; Other Marketplace _____

List Price Chosen _____    Currency _____

Rate _____    Delivery _____    Royalty _____


&ast; Other Marketplace _____

List Price Chosen _____    Currency _____

Rate _____    Delivery _____    Royalty _____


&ast; Other Marketplace _____

List Price Chosen _____    Currency _____

Rate _____    Delivery _____    Royalty _____


&ast; Other Marketplace _____

List Price Chosen _____    Currency _____

Rate _____    Delivery _____    Royalty _____


&ast; Other Marketplace _____

List Price Chosen _____    Currency _____

Rate _____    Delivery _____    Royalty _____


&ast; Other Marketplace _____

List Price Chosen _____    Currency _____

Rate _____    Delivery _____    Royalty _____


&ast; Other Marketplace _____

List Price Chosen _____    Currency _____

Rate _____    Delivery _____    Royalty _____

**Book Title** _____

Matchbook

____ Enroll my book in Kindle Matchbook

Book Lending

____ Allow Kindle Book Lending

Terms & Conditions ____ Read

Save as Draft Date _____

Clicked Publish Your Kindle eBook Date _____

Published Notice from KDP Date _____

## Note Date & Changes Made

_____

_____

_____

_____

_____

_____

_____

_____

_____

_____

_____

_____

_____

_____

_____

**Book Title** _____

## Note Date & Changes Made

_____

_____

_____

_____

_____

_____

_____

_____

_____

_____

_____

_____

_____

_____

_____

_____

_____

_____

_____

_____

_____

# BOOK 4 - Date _____

## Kindle eBook Details

Language _____

Book Title _____

Subtitle _____

Series _____ # _____

Edition Number (optional) _____

Author _____

Contributors (opt) _____

_____

_____

_____

Description: _____

_____

_____

_____

_____

_____

_____

_____

_____

_____

_____

_____

_____

Publishing Rights (circle or underline one)

    I own the copyright

    This is a public domain work

**Book Title** _____

Keywords (seven words or phrases)

_____

_____

_____

_____

_____

_____

_____

Categories (two)

_____

_____

_____

_____

Age & Grade Range

Children's Book age range (optional)

    Minimum \_\_\_\_        Maximum \_\_\_\_

U.S. grade range

    Minimum \_\_\_\_        Maximum \_\_\_\_

Adult Content        No    Yes

## Kindle eBook Content

Manuscript

    Digital Rights Management (DRM)

    Enable DRM on this Kindle eBooks?

        Yes \_\_\_\_      No \_\_\_\_

**Book Title** _____

Recommended formats for Kindle eBooks:

.doc, .docx, HTML, MOBI, ePub, RTF, Plain Text, and KPF.

Upload eBook manuscript

File name _____

Uploaded      Date _____

Spell Check

     ("Ignore All" doesn't always work)

File Updated     Date _____

File Updated     Date _____

File Updated     Date _____

**Interior Formatter** _____

Contact Info: _____

Cost: _____


Kindle eBook Cover (check one)

    ___ Use Cover Creator to make your book cover

    ___ Upload a cover you already have (JPG/TIFF only)


Upload your cover file

File name _____

Uploaded      Date _____

Kindle eBook Preview via Online Previewer

    ___ Launch Previewer    Approved date: _____

Downloadable Preview Options

    ___ On your computer    ___ On your Kindle device

**Book Title** _____

    Cover Updated   Date _____

    Cover Updated   Date _____

    Cover Updated   Date _____

    **Cover Designer** _____

    Contact Info: _____

    Cost: _____

ISBN (Optional Choice)

    Kindle ISBN _____

    Your ISBN _____

    Publisher (optional) _____

## Kindle eBook Pricing

KDP Select Enrollment (Optional)   Yes ____     No ____

Territories (check one)

    ____ All territories

    ____ Individual territories (Note all your choices below)

_____

_____

_____

_____

_____

_____

_____

_____

_____

**Book Title** _____

Royalty & Pricing - Select a royalty plan and set your Kindle eBook list prices below.

___ 30%          ___ 70%

Your book file size after conversion is _____

Primary Marketplace _____

List Price Chosen _____          Currency _____

Rate _____          Delivery _____          Royalty _____


* Other Marketplace _____

List Price Chosen _____          Currency _____

Rate _____          Delivery _____          Royalty _____


* Other Marketplace _____

List Price Chosen _____          Currency _____

Rate _____          Delivery _____          Royalty _____


* Other Marketplace _____

List Price Chosen _____          Currency _____

Rate _____          Delivery _____          Royalty _____


* Other Marketplace _____

List Price Chosen _____          Currency _____

Rate _____          Delivery _____          Royalty _____


* Other Marketplace _____

List Price Chosen _____          Currency _____

Rate _____          Delivery _____          Royalty _____

**Book Title** _____

* Other Marketplace _____

List Price Chosen _____ Currency _____

Rate _____ Delivery _____ Royalty _____


* Other Marketplace _____

List Price Chosen _____ Currency _____

Rate _____ Delivery _____ Royalty _____


* Other Marketplace _____

List Price Chosen _____ Currency _____

Rate _____ Delivery _____ Royalty _____


* Other Marketplace _____

List Price Chosen _____ Currency _____

Rate _____ Delivery _____ Royalty _____


* Other Marketplace _____

List Price Chosen _____ Currency _____

Rate _____ Delivery _____ Royalty _____


* Other Marketplace _____

List Price Chosen _____ Currency _____

Rate _____ Delivery _____ Royalty _____


* Other Marketplace _____

List Price Chosen _____ Currency _____

Rate _____ Delivery _____ Royalty _____

**Book Title** _____

Matchbook

    ___ Enroll my book in Kindle Matchbook

Book Lending

    ___ Allow Kindle Book Lending

Terms & Conditions ___ Read

    Save as Draft Date _____

    Clicked Publish Your Kindle eBook Date _____

    Published Notice from KDP Date _____

## Note Date & Changes Made

_____

_____

_____

_____

_____

_____

_____

_____

_____

_____

_____

_____

_____

_____

_____

_____

**Book Title** _____

## Note Date & Changes Made

_____

_____

_____

_____

_____

_____

_____

_____

_____

_____

_____

_____

_____

_____

_____

_____

_____

_____

_____

_____

_____

_____

_____

_____

# BOOK 5 - Date _____

## Kindle eBook Details

Language _____

Book Title _____

Subtitle _____

Series _____ # ____

Edition Number (optional) _____

Author _____

Contributors (opt) _____

_____

_____

_____

Description: _____

_____

_____

_____

_____

_____

_____

_____

_____

_____

_____

_____

Publishing Rights (circle or underline one)

I own the copyright

This is a public domain work

**Book Title** _____

Keywords (seven words or phrases)

_____

_____

_____

_____

_____

_____

_____

Categories (two)

_____

_____

_____

_____

Age & Grade Range

Children's Book age range (optional)

    Minimum _____        Maximum _____

U.S. grade range

    Minimum _____        Maximum _____

Adult Content        No      Yes

## Kindle eBook Content

Manuscript

    Digital Rights Management (DRM)

    Enable DRM on this Kindle eBooks?

        Yes _____     No _____

**Book Title** _____

Recommended formats for Kindle eBooks:

.doc, .docx, HTML, MOBI, ePub, RTF, Plain Text, and KPF.

Upload eBook manuscript

File name _____

Uploaded          Date _____

Spell Check

    ("Ignore All" doesn't always work)

File Updated      Date _____

File Updated      Date _____

File Updated      Date _____

**Interior Formatter** _____

Contact Info: _____

Cost: _____

Kindle eBook Cover (check one)

    ___ Use Cover Creator to make your book cover

    ___ Upload a cover you already have (JPG/TIFF only)

Upload your cover file

File name _____

Uploaded          Date _____

Kindle eBook Preview via Online Previewer

    ___ Launch Previewer      Approved date: _____

Downloadable Preview Options

    ___ On your computer        ___ On your Kindle device

**Book Title** _____

    Cover Updated    Date _____

    Cover Updated    Date _____

    Cover Updated    Date _____

    **Cover Designer** _____

    Contact Info: _____

    Cost: _____

ISBN (Optional Choice)

    Kindle ISBN _____

    Your ISBN _____

    Publisher (optional) _____

## Kindle eBook Pricing

KDP Select Enrollment (Optional)    Yes ____    No ____

Territories (check one)

    ____ All territories

    ____ Individual territories (Note all your choices below)

_____

_____

_____

_____

_____

_____

_____

_____

_____

**Book Title** _____

Royalty & Pricing - Select a royalty plan and set your Kindle eBook list prices below.

   ___ 30%      ___ 70%

Your book file size after conversion is _____

Primary Marketplace _____

List Price Chosen _____    Currency _____

Rate _____  Delivery _____  Royalty _____


* Other Marketplace _____

List Price Chosen _____    Currency _____

Rate _____  Delivery _____  Royalty _____


* Other Marketplace _____

List Price Chosen _____    Currency _____

Rate _____  Delivery _____  Royalty _____


* Other Marketplace _____

List Price Chosen _____    Currency _____

Rate _____  Delivery _____  Royalty _____


* Other Marketplace _____

List Price Chosen _____    Currency _____

Rate _____  Delivery _____  Royalty _____


* Other Marketplace _____

List Price Chosen _____    Currency _____

Rate _____  Delivery _____  Royalty _____

**Book Title** _____

* Other Marketplace _____

List Price Chosen _____ Currency _____

Rate _____ Delivery _____ Royalty _____

* Other Marketplace _____

List Price Chosen _____ Currency _____

Rate _____ Delivery _____ Royalty _____

* Other Marketplace _____

List Price Chosen _____ Currency _____

Rate _____ Delivery _____ Royalty _____

* Other Marketplace _____

List Price Chosen _____ Currency _____

Rate _____ Delivery _____ Royalty _____

* Other Marketplace _____

List Price Chosen _____ Currency _____

Rate _____ Delivery _____ Royalty _____

* Other Marketplace _____

List Price Chosen _____ Currency _____

Rate _____ Delivery _____ Royalty _____

* Other Marketplace _____

List Price Chosen _____ Currency _____

Rate _____ Delivery _____ Royalty _____

**Book Title** _____

Matchbook

    ___ Enroll my book in Kindle Matchbook

Book Lending

    ___ Allow Kindle Book Lending

Terms & Conditions ___ Read

    Save as Draft Date _____

    Clicked Publish Your Kindle eBook Date _____

    Published Notice from KDP Date _____

## Note Date & Changes Made

_____

_____

_____

_____

_____

_____

_____

_____

_____

_____

_____

_____

_____

_____

_____

_____

**Book Title** _____

## Note Date & Changes Made

_____

_____

_____

_____

_____

_____

_____

_____

_____

_____

_____

_____

_____

_____

_____

_____

_____

_____

_____

_____

_____

_____

_____

# BOOK 6 - Date _____

## Kindle eBook Details

Language _____

Book Title _____

Subtitle _____

Series _____ # \_\_\_\_

Edition Number (optional) \_\_\_\_\_

Author _____

Contributors (opt) _____

_____

_____

_____

Description: _____

_____

_____

_____

_____

_____

_____

_____

_____

_____

_____

Publishing Rights (circle or underline one)

        I own the copyright

        This is a public domain work

**Book Title** _____

    Keywords (seven words or phrases)

    _____

    _____

    _____

    _____

    _____

    _____

    _____

    Categories (two)

    _____

    _____

    _____

    _____

    Age & Grade Range

    Children's Book age range (optional)

        Minimum ____        Maximum ____

    U.S. grade range

        Minimum ____        Maximum ____

    Adult Content        No    Yes

## Kindle eBook Content

Manuscript

    Digital Rights Management (DRM)

    Enable DRM on this Kindle eBooks?

        Yes ____    No ____

**Book Title** _____

Recommended formats for Kindle eBooks:
.doc, .docx, HTML, MOBI, ePub, RTF, Plain Text, and KPF.

Upload eBook manuscript
File name _____
Uploaded          Date _____
Spell Check
    ("Ignore All" doesn't always work)

File Updated      Date _____
File Updated      Date _____
File Updated      Date _____
**Interior Formatter** _____
Contact Info: _____
Cost: _____

Kindle eBook Cover (check one)
    ____ Use Cover Creator to make your book cover
    ____ Upload a cover you already have (JPG/TIFF only)

Upload your cover file
File name _____
Uploaded          Date _____
Kindle eBook Preview via Online Previewer
    ____ Launch Previewer       Approved date: _____
Downloadable Preview Options
    ____ On your computer        ____ On your Kindle device

**Book Title** _____

    Cover Updated   Date _____

    Cover Updated   Date _____

    Cover Updated   Date _____

    **Cover Designer** _____

    Contact Info: _____

    Cost: _____

ISBN (Optional Choice)

    Kindle ISBN _____

    Your ISBN _____

    Publisher (optional) _____

## Kindle eBook Pricing

KDP Select Enrollment (Optional)   Yes ___     No ___

Territories (check one)

    ___ All territories

    ___ Individual territories (Note all your choices below)

_____

_____

_____

_____

_____

_____

_____

_____

_____

**Book Title** _____

Royalty & Pricing - Select a royalty plan and set your Kindle eBook list prices below.

_____ 30%      _____ 70%

Your book file size after conversion is _____

Primary Marketplace _____

List Price Chosen _____    Currency _____

Rate _____    Delivery _____    Royalty _____


* Other Marketplace _____

List Price Chosen _____    Currency _____

Rate _____    Delivery _____    Royalty _____


* Other Marketplace _____

List Price Chosen _____    Currency _____

Rate _____    Delivery _____    Royalty _____


* Other Marketplace _____

List Price Chosen _____    Currency _____

Rate _____    Delivery _____    Royalty _____


* Other Marketplace _____

List Price Chosen _____    Currency _____

Rate _____    Delivery _____    Royalty _____


* Other Marketplace _____

List Price Chosen _____    Currency _____

Rate _____    Delivery _____    Royalty _____

**Book Title** _____

\* Other Marketplace _____

List Price Chosen _____     Currency _____

Rate _____     Delivery _____     Royalty _____


\* Other Marketplace _____

List Price Chosen _____     Currency _____

Rate _____     Delivery _____     Royalty _____


\* Other Marketplace _____

List Price Chosen _____     Currency _____

Rate _____     Delivery _____     Royalty _____


\* Other Marketplace _____

List Price Chosen _____     Currency _____

Rate _____     Delivery _____     Royalty _____


\* Other Marketplace _____

List Price Chosen _____     Currency _____

Rate _____     Delivery _____     Royalty _____


\* Other Marketplace _____

List Price Chosen _____     Currency _____

Rate _____     Delivery _____     Royalty _____


\* Other Marketplace _____

List Price Chosen _____     Currency _____

Rate _____     Delivery _____     Royalty _____

**Book Title** _____

Matchbook

_____ Enroll my book in Kindle Matchbook

Book Lending

_____ Allow Kindle Book Lending

Terms & Conditions _____ Read

Save as Draft Date _____

Clicked Publish Your Kindle eBook Date _____

Published Notice from KDP Date _____

## Note Date & Changes Made

_____

_____

_____

_____

_____

_____

_____

_____

_____

_____

_____

_____

_____

_____

_____

_____

_____

**Book Title** _____

## Note Date & Changes Made

_____

_____

_____

_____

_____

_____

_____

_____

_____

_____

_____

_____

_____

_____

_____

_____

_____

_____

_____

_____

_____

_____

_____

# BOOK 7 - Date _____

## Kindle eBook Details

Language _____

Book Title _____

Subtitle _____

Series _____ # _____

Edition Number (optional) _____

Author _____

Contributors (opt) _____

_____

_____

_____

Description: _____

_____

_____

_____

_____

_____

_____

_____

_____

_____

_____

_____

_____

Publishing Rights (circle or underline one)

I own the copyright

This is a public domain work

**Book Title** _____

Keywords (seven words or phrases)

_____

_____

_____

_____

_____

_____

_____

Categories (two)

_____

_____

_____

_____

Age & Grade Range

Children's Book age range (optional)

    Minimum _____           Maximum _____

U.S. grade range

    Minimum _____           Maximum _____

Adult Content         No    Yes

## Kindle eBook Content

Manuscript

    Digital Rights Management (DRM)

    Enable DRM on this Kindle eBooks?

        Yes _____     No _____

**Book Title** _____

Recommended formats for Kindle eBooks:
.doc, .docx, HTML, MOBI, ePub, RTF, Plain Text, and KPF.

Upload eBook manuscript

File name _____

Uploaded          Date _____

Spell Check

    ("Ignore All" doesn't always work)

File Updated          Date _____

File Updated          Date _____

File Updated          Date _____

**Interior Formatter** _____

Contact Info: _____

Cost: _____

Kindle eBook Cover (check one)

    ___ Use Cover Creator to make your book cover

    ___ Upload a cover you already have (JPG/TIFF only)

Upload your cover file

File name _____

Uploaded          Date _____

Kindle eBook Preview via Online Previewer

    ___ Launch Previewer          Approved date: _____

Downloadable Preview Options

    ___ On your computer          ___ On your Kindle device

**Book Title** _____

    Cover Updated   Date _____

    Cover Updated   Date _____

    Cover Updated   Date _____

    **Cover Designer** _____

    Contact Info: _____

    Cost: _____

ISBN (Optional Choice)

    Kindle ISBN _____

    Your ISBN _____

    Publisher (optional) _____

## Kindle eBook Pricing

KDP Select Enrollment (Optional)   Yes ____    No ____

Territories (check one)

    ____ All territories

    ____ Individual territories (Note all your choices below)

_____

_____

_____

_____

_____

_____

_____

_____

_____

**Book Title** _____

Royalty & Pricing - Select a royalty plan and set your Kindle eBook list prices below.

_____ 30%          _____ 70%

Your book file size after conversion is _____

Primary Marketplace _____

List Price Chosen _____          Currency _____

Rate _____   Delivery _____   Royalty _____


* Other Marketplace _____

List Price Chosen _____          Currency _____

Rate _____   Delivery _____   Royalty _____


* Other Marketplace _____

List Price Chosen _____          Currency _____

Rate _____   Delivery _____   Royalty _____


* Other Marketplace _____

List Price Chosen _____          Currency _____

Rate _____   Delivery _____   Royalty _____


* Other Marketplace _____

List Price Chosen _____          Currency _____

Rate _____   Delivery _____   Royalty _____


* Other Marketplace _____

List Price Chosen _____          Currency _____

Rate _____   Delivery _____   Royalty _____

**Book Title** _____

* Other Marketplace _____

List Price Chosen _____ Currency _____

Rate _____ Delivery _____ Royalty _____


* Other Marketplace _____

List Price Chosen _____ Currency _____

Rate _____ Delivery _____ Royalty _____


* Other Marketplace _____

List Price Chosen _____ Currency _____

Rate _____ Delivery _____ Royalty _____


* Other Marketplace _____

List Price Chosen _____ Currency _____

Rate _____ Delivery _____ Royalty _____


* Other Marketplace _____

List Price Chosen _____ Currency _____

Rate _____ Delivery _____ Royalty _____


* Other Marketplace _____

List Price Chosen _____ Currency _____

Rate _____ Delivery _____ Royalty _____


* Other Marketplace _____

List Price Chosen _____ Currency _____

Rate _____ Delivery _____ Royalty _____

**Book Title** _____

Matchbook

___ Enroll my book in Kindle Matchbook

Book Lending

___ Allow Kindle Book Lending

Terms & Conditions ___ Read

Save as Draft Date _____

Clicked Publish Your Kindle eBook Date _____

Published Notice from KDP Date _____

## Note Date & Changes Made

_____

_____

_____

_____

_____

_____

_____

_____

_____

_____

_____

_____

_____

_____

_____

**Book Title** _____

## Note Date & Changes Made

_____
_____
_____
_____
_____
_____
_____
_____
_____
_____
_____
_____
_____
_____
_____
_____
_____
_____
_____
_____
_____
_____
_____

# BOOK 8 - Date _____

## Kindle eBook Details

Language _____

Book Title _____

Subtitle _____

Series _____ # _____

Edition Number (optional) _____

Author _____

Contributors (opt) _____

_____

_____

_____

Description: _____

_____

_____

_____

_____

_____

_____

_____

_____

_____

_____

_____

_____

Publishing Rights (circle or underline one)

       I own the copyright

       This is a public domain work

**Book Title** _____

Keywords (seven words or phrases)

_____

_____

_____

_____

_____

_____

_____

Categories (two)

_____

_____

_____

Age & Grade Range

Children's Book age range (optional)

    Minimum _____           Maximum _____

U.S. grade range

    Minimum _____           Maximum _____

Adult Content        No    Yes

## Kindle eBook Content

Manuscript

    Digital Rights Management (DRM)

    Enable DRM on this Kindle eBooks?

        Yes _____      No _____

**Book Title** _____

Recommended formats for Kindle eBooks:

.doc, .docx, HTML, MOBI, ePub, RTF, Plain Text, and KPF.

Upload eBook manuscript

File name _____

Uploaded          Date _____

Spell Check

    ("Ignore All" doesn't always work)

File Updated      Date _____

File Updated      Date _____

File Updated      Date _____

**Interior Formatter** _____

Contact Info: _____

Cost: _____

Kindle eBook Cover (check one)

    ___ Use Cover Creator to make your book cover

    ___ Upload a cover you already have (JPG/TIFF only)

Upload your cover file

File name _____

Uploaded          Date _____

Kindle eBook Preview via Online Previewer

    ___ Launch Previewer          Approved date: _____

Downloadable Preview Options

    ___ On your computer          ___ On your Kindle device

**Book Title** _____

    Cover Updated   Date _____

    Cover Updated   Date _____

    Cover Updated   Date _____

    **Cover Designer** _____

    Contact Info: _____

    Cost: _____

ISBN (Optional Choice)

    Kindle ISBN _____

    Your ISBN _____

    Publisher (optional) _____


**Kindle eBook Pricing**

KDP Select Enrollment (Optional)   Yes ___    No ___


Territories (check one)

    ___ All territories

    ___ Individual territories (Note all your choices below)

_____

_____

_____

_____

_____

_____

_____

_____

**Book Title** _____

Royalty & Pricing - Select a royalty plan and set your Kindle eBook list prices below.

_____ 30%        _____ 70%

Your book file size after conversion is _____

Primary Marketplace _____

List Price Chosen _____    Currency _____

Rate _____    Delivery _____    Royalty _____


\* Other Marketplace _____

List Price Chosen _____    Currency _____

Rate _____    Delivery _____    Royalty _____


\* Other Marketplace _____

List Price Chosen _____    Currency _____

Rate _____    Delivery _____    Royalty _____


\* Other Marketplace _____

List Price Chosen _____    Currency _____

Rate _____    Delivery _____    Royalty _____


\* Other Marketplace _____

List Price Chosen _____    Currency _____

Rate _____    Delivery _____    Royalty _____


\* Other Marketplace _____

List Price Chosen _____    Currency _____

Rate _____    Delivery _____    Royalty _____

**Book Title** _____

* Other Marketplace _____

List Price Chosen _____ Currency _____

Rate _____ Delivery _____ Royalty _____


* Other Marketplace _____

List Price Chosen _____ Currency _____

Rate _____ Delivery _____ Royalty _____


* Other Marketplace _____

List Price Chosen _____ Currency _____

Rate _____ Delivery _____ Royalty _____


* Other Marketplace _____

List Price Chosen _____ Currency _____

Rate _____ Delivery _____ Royalty _____


* Other Marketplace _____

List Price Chosen _____ Currency _____

Rate _____ Delivery _____ Royalty _____


* Other Marketplace _____

List Price Chosen _____ Currency _____

Rate _____ Delivery _____ Royalty _____


* Other Marketplace _____

List Price Chosen _____ Currency _____

Rate _____ Delivery _____ Royalty _____

**Book Title** _____

Matchbook

_____ Enroll my book in Kindle Matchbook

Book Lending

_____ Allow Kindle Book Lending

Terms & Conditions _____ Read

Save as Draft Date _____

Clicked Publish Your Kindle eBook Date _____

Published Notice from KDP Date _____

## Note Date & Changes Made

_____

_____

_____

_____

_____

_____

_____

_____

_____

_____

_____

_____

_____

_____

_____

_____

_____

**Book Title** _____

## Note Date & Changes Made

_____

_____

_____

_____

_____

_____

_____

_____

_____

_____

_____

_____

_____

_____

_____

_____

_____

_____

_____

_____

_____

_____

_____

# BOOK 9 - Date _____

## Kindle eBook Details

Language _____

Book Title _____

Subtitle _____

Series _____ # _____

Edition Number (optional) _____

Author _____

Contributors (opt) _____

_____

_____

_____

Description: _____

_____

_____

_____

_____

_____

_____

_____

_____

_____

_____

_____

Publishing Rights (circle or underline one)

        I own the copyright

        This is a public domain work

**Book Title** _____

    Keywords (seven words or phrases)

    _____

    _____

    _____

    _____

    _____

    _____

    _____

    Categories (two)

    _____

    _____

    _____

    _____

    Age & Grade Range

    Children's Book age range (optional)

        Minimum _____        Maximum _____

    U.S. grade range

        Minimum _____        Maximum _____

    Adult Content        No    Yes

## Kindle eBook Content

Manuscript

    Digital Rights Management (DRM)

    Enable DRM on this Kindle eBooks?

        Yes _____       No _____

**Book Title** _____

Recommended formats for Kindle eBooks:
.doc, .docx, HTML, MOBI, ePub, RTF, Plain Text, and KPF.

Upload eBook manuscript
File name _____
Uploaded          Date _____
Spell Check
        ("Ignore All" doesn't always work)

File Updated      Date _____
File Updated      Date _____
File Updated      Date _____
**Interior Formatter** _____
Contact Info: _____
Cost: _____

Kindle eBook Cover (check one)
        ___ Use Cover Creator to make your book cover
        ___ Upload a cover you already have (JPG/TIFF only)

Upload your cover file
File name _____
Uploaded          Date _____
Kindle eBook Preview via Online Previewer
        ___ Launch Previewer          Approved date: _____
Downloadable Preview Options
        ___ On your computer          ___ On your Kindle device

**Book Title** _____

    Cover Updated    Date _____

    Cover Updated    Date _____

    Cover Updated    Date _____

    **Cover Designer** _____

    Contact Info: _____

    Cost: _____

ISBN (Optional Choice)

    Kindle ISBN _____

    Your ISBN _____

    Publisher (optional) _____

## Kindle eBook Pricing

KDP Select Enrollment (Optional)    Yes ___    No ___

Territories (check one)

    ___ All territories

    ___ Individual territories (Note all your choices below)

_____

_____

_____

_____

_____

_____

_____

_____

**Book Title** _____

Royalty & Pricing - Select a royalty plan and set your Kindle
eBook list prices below.

   ___ 30%      ___ 70%

Your book file size after conversion is _____

Primary Marketplace _____

List Price Chosen _____    Currency _____

Rate _____   Delivery _____   Royalty _____


* Other Marketplace _____

List Price Chosen _____    Currency _____

Rate _____   Delivery _____   Royalty _____


* Other Marketplace _____

List Price Chosen _____    Currency _____

Rate _____   Delivery _____   Royalty _____


* Other Marketplace _____

List Price Chosen _____    Currency _____

Rate _____   Delivery _____   Royalty _____


* Other Marketplace _____

List Price Chosen _____    Currency _____

Rate _____   Delivery _____   Royalty _____


* Other Marketplace _____

List Price Chosen _____    Currency _____

Rate _____   Delivery _____   Royalty _____

**Book Title** _____

* Other Marketplace _____

List Price Chosen _____     Currency _____

Rate _____     Delivery _____     Royalty _____


* Other Marketplace _____

List Price Chosen _____     Currency _____

Rate _____     Delivery _____     Royalty _____


* Other Marketplace _____

List Price Chosen _____     Currency _____

Rate _____     Delivery _____     Royalty _____


* Other Marketplace _____

List Price Chosen _____     Currency _____

Rate _____     Delivery _____     Royalty _____


* Other Marketplace _____

List Price Chosen _____     Currency _____

Rate _____     Delivery _____     Royalty _____


* Other Marketplace _____

List Price Chosen _____     Currency _____

Rate _____     Delivery _____     Royalty _____


* Other Marketplace _____

List Price Chosen _____     Currency _____

Rate _____     Delivery _____     Royalty _____

**Book Title** _____

Matchbook

    ___ Enroll my book in Kindle Matchbook

Book Lending

    ___ Allow Kindle Book Lending

Terms & Conditions ___ Read

    Save as Draft Date _____

    Clicked Publish Your Kindle eBook Date _____

    Published Notice from KDP Date _____

## Note Date & Changes Made

_____

_____

_____

_____

_____

_____

_____

_____

_____

_____

_____

_____

_____

_____

_____

_____

**Book Title** _____

## Note Date & Changes Made

_____

_____

_____

_____

_____

_____

_____

_____

_____

_____

_____

_____

_____

_____

_____

_____

_____

_____

_____

_____

_____

_____

_____

_____

# BOOK 10 - Date _____

## Kindle eBook Details

Language _____

Book Title _____

Subtitle _____

Series _____ # _____

Edition Number (optional) _____

Author _____

Contributors (opt) _____

_____

_____

_____

Description: _____

_____

_____

_____

_____

_____

_____

_____

_____

_____

_____

_____

Publishing Rights (circle or underline one)

        I own the copyright

        This is a public domain work

**Book Title** _____

Keywords (seven words or phrases)

_____

_____

_____

_____

_____

_____

_____

Categories (two)

_____

_____

_____

Age & Grade Range

Children's Book age range (optional)

    Minimum ____             Maximum ____

U.S. grade range

    Minimum ____             Maximum ____

Adult Content           No     Yes

## Kindle eBook Content

Manuscript

    Digital Rights Management (DRM)

    Enable DRM on this Kindle eBooks?

        Yes ____       No ____

**Book Title** _____

Recommended formats for Kindle eBooks:
.doc, .docx, HTML, MOBI, ePub, RTF, Plain Text, and KPF.

Upload eBook manuscript
File name _____
Uploaded          Date _____
Spell Check
    ("Ignore All" doesn't always work)

File Updated      Date _____
File Updated      Date _____
File Updated      Date _____
**Interior Formatter** _____
Contact Info: _____
Cost: _____

Kindle eBook Cover (check one)
    ___ Use Cover Creator to make your book cover
    ___ Upload a cover you already have (JPG/TIFF only)

Upload your cover file
File name _____
Uploaded          Date _____
Kindle eBook Preview via Online Previewer
    ___ Launch Previewer          Approved date: _____
Downloadable Preview Options
    ___ On your computer          ___ On your Kindle device

**Book Title** _____

    Cover Updated   Date _____

    Cover Updated   Date _____

    Cover Updated   Date _____

    **Cover Designer** _____

    Contact Info: _____

    Cost: _____

ISBN (Optional Choice)

    Kindle ISBN _____

    Your ISBN _____

    Publisher (optional) _____

## Kindle eBook Pricing

KDP Select Enrollment (Optional)    Yes ____    No ____

Territories (check one)

    ____ All territories

    ____ Individual territories (Note all your choices below)

_____

_____

_____

_____

_____

_____

_____

_____

_____

**Book Title** _____

Royalty & Pricing - Select a royalty plan and set your Kindle eBook list prices below.

_____ 30%          _____ 70%

Your book file size after conversion is _____

Primary Marketplace _____

List Price Chosen _____          Currency _____

Rate _____          Delivery _____          Royalty _____


* Other Marketplace _____

List Price Chosen _____          Currency _____

Rate _____          Delivery _____          Royalty _____


* Other Marketplace _____

List Price Chosen _____          Currency _____

Rate _____          Delivery _____          Royalty _____


* Other Marketplace _____

List Price Chosen _____          Currency _____

Rate _____          Delivery _____          Royalty _____


* Other Marketplace _____

List Price Chosen _____          Currency _____

Rate _____          Delivery _____          Royalty _____


* Other Marketplace _____

List Price Chosen _____          Currency _____

Rate _____          Delivery _____          Royalty _____

**Book Title** _____

* Other Marketplace _____

List Price Chosen _____ Currency _____

Rate _____ Delivery _____ Royalty _____


* Other Marketplace _____

List Price Chosen _____ Currency _____

Rate _____ Delivery _____ Royalty _____


* Other Marketplace _____

List Price Chosen _____ Currency _____

Rate _____ Delivery _____ Royalty _____


* Other Marketplace _____

List Price Chosen _____ Currency _____

Rate _____ Delivery _____ Royalty _____


* Other Marketplace _____

List Price Chosen _____ Currency _____

Rate _____ Delivery _____ Royalty _____


* Other Marketplace _____

List Price Chosen _____ Currency _____

Rate _____ Delivery _____ Royalty _____


* Other Marketplace _____

List Price Chosen _____ Currency _____

Rate _____ Delivery _____ Royalty _____

**Book Title** _____

Matchbook

_____ Enroll my book in Kindle Matchbook

Book Lending

_____ Allow Kindle Book Lending

Terms & Conditions _____ Read

Save as Draft Date _____

Clicked Publish Your Kindle eBook Date _____

Published Notice from KDP Date _____

## Note Date & Changes Made

_____

_____

_____

_____

_____

_____

_____

_____

_____

_____

_____

_____

_____

_____

_____

**Book Title** _____

## Note Date & Changes Made

_____

_____

_____

_____

_____

_____

_____

_____

_____

_____

_____

_____

_____

_____

_____

_____

_____

_____

_____

_____

_____

_____

_____

_____

# BOOK 11 - Date _____

## Kindle eBook Details

Language _____

Book Title _____

Subtitle _____

Series _____ # _____

Edition Number (optional) _____

Author _____

Contributors (opt) _____

_____

_____

Description: _____

_____

_____

_____

_____

_____

_____

_____

_____

_____

_____

_____

Publishing Rights (circle or underline one)

I own the copyright

This is a public domain work

**Book Title** _____

Keywords (seven words or phrases)

_____

_____

_____

_____

_____

_____

_____

Categories (two)

_____

_____

_____

_____

Age & Grade Range

Children's Book age range (optional)

    Minimum _____          Maximum _____

U.S. grade range

    Minimum _____          Maximum _____

Adult Content         No    Yes

## Kindle eBook Content

Manuscript

    Digital Rights Management (DRM)

    Enable DRM on this Kindle eBooks?

        Yes _____     No _____

**Book Title** _____

Recommended formats for Kindle eBooks:

.doc, .docx, HTML, MOBI, ePub, RTF, Plain Text, and KPF.

Upload eBook manuscript

File name _____

Uploaded          Date _____

Spell Check

    ("Ignore All" doesn't always work)

File Updated     Date _____

File Updated     Date _____

File Updated     Date _____

**Interior Formatter** _____

Contact Info: _____

Cost: _____

Kindle eBook Cover (check one)

    ___ Use Cover Creator to make your book cover

    ___ Upload a cover you already have (JPG/TIFF only)

Upload your cover file

File name _____

Uploaded          Date _____

Kindle eBook Preview via Online Previewer

    ___ Launch Previewer          Approved date: _____

Downloadable Preview Options

    ___ On your computer          ___ On your Kindle device

**Book Title** _____

    Cover Updated   Date _____

    Cover Updated   Date _____

    Cover Updated   Date _____

    **Cover Designer** _____

    Contact Info: _____

    Cost: _____

ISBN (Optional Choice)

    Kindle ISBN _____

    Your ISBN _____

    Publisher (optional) _____

## Kindle eBook Pricing

KDP Select Enrollment (Optional)   Yes ___    No ___

Territories (check one)

    ___ All territories

    ___ Individual territories (Note all your choices below)

_____

_____

_____

_____

_____

_____

_____

_____

**Book Title** _____

Royalty & Pricing - Select a royalty plan and set your Kindle eBook list prices below.

_____ 30%          _____ 70%

Your book file size after conversion is _____

Primary Marketplace _____

List Price Chosen _____     Currency _____

Rate _____   Delivery _____   Royalty _____


* Other Marketplace _____

List Price Chosen _____     Currency _____

Rate _____   Delivery _____   Royalty _____


* Other Marketplace _____

List Price Chosen _____     Currency _____

Rate _____   Delivery _____   Royalty _____


* Other Marketplace _____

List Price Chosen _____     Currency _____

Rate _____   Delivery _____   Royalty _____


* Other Marketplace _____

List Price Chosen _____     Currency _____

Rate _____   Delivery _____   Royalty _____


* Other Marketplace _____

List Price Chosen _____     Currency _____

Rate _____   Delivery _____   Royalty _____

**Book Title** _____

* Other Marketplace _____

List Price Chosen _____     Currency _____

Rate _____    Delivery _____    Royalty _____


* Other Marketplace _____

List Price Chosen _____     Currency _____

Rate _____    Delivery _____    Royalty _____


* Other Marketplace _____

List Price Chosen _____     Currency _____

Rate _____    Delivery _____    Royalty _____


* Other Marketplace _____

List Price Chosen _____     Currency _____

Rate _____    Delivery _____    Royalty _____


* Other Marketplace _____

List Price Chosen _____     Currency _____

Rate _____    Delivery _____    Royalty _____


* Other Marketplace _____

List Price Chosen _____     Currency _____

Rate _____    Delivery _____    Royalty _____


* Other Marketplace _____

List Price Chosen _____     Currency _____

Rate _____    Delivery _____    Royalty _____

**Book Title** _____

Matchbook

    ___ Enroll my book in Kindle Matchbook

Book Lending

    ___ Allow Kindle Book Lending

Terms & Conditions ___ Read

    Save as Draft Date _____

    Clicked Publish Your Kindle eBook Date _____

    Published Notice from KDP Date _____

## Note Date & Changes Made

_____

_____

_____

_____

_____

_____

_____

_____

_____

_____

_____

_____

_____

_____

_____

_____

**Book Title** _____

## Note Date & Changes Made

_____

_____

_____

_____

_____

_____

_____

_____

_____

_____

_____

_____

_____

_____

_____

_____

_____

_____

_____

_____

_____

_____

_____

# BOOK 12 - Date _____

## Kindle eBook Details

Language _____

Book Title _____

Subtitle _____

Series _____ # ____

Edition Number (optional) _____

Author _____

Contributors (opt) _____

_____

_____

_____

Description: _____

_____

_____

_____

_____

_____

_____

_____

_____

_____

_____

_____

Publishing Rights (circle or underline one)

      I own the copyright

      This is a public domain work

**Book Title** _____

Keywords (seven words or phrases)

_____

_____

_____

_____

_____

_____

_____

Categories (two)

_____

_____

_____

Age & Grade Range

Children's Book age range (optional)

    Minimum _____           Maximum _____

U.S. grade range

    Minimum _____           Maximum _____

Adult Content        No    Yes

## Kindle eBook Content

Manuscript

    Digital Rights Management (DRM)

    Enable DRM on this Kindle eBooks?

        Yes _____        No _____

**Book Title** _____

Recommended formats for Kindle eBooks:

.doc, .docx, HTML, MOBI, ePub, RTF, Plain Text, and KPF.

Upload eBook manuscript

File name _____

Uploaded          Date _____

Spell Check

    ("Ignore All" doesn't always work)

File Updated      Date _____

File Updated      Date _____

File Updated      Date _____

**Interior Formatter** _____

Contact Info: _____

Cost: _____

Kindle eBook Cover (check one)

    ____ Use Cover Creator to make your book cover

    ____ Upload a cover you already have (JPG/TIFF only)

Upload your cover file

File name _____

Uploaded          Date _____

Kindle eBook Preview via Online Previewer

    ____ Launch Previewer          Approved date: _____

Downloadable Preview Options

    ____ On your computer          ____ On your Kindle device

**Book Title** _____

      Cover Updated   Date _____

      Cover Updated   Date _____

      Cover Updated   Date _____

      **Cover Designer** _____

      Contact Info: _____

      Cost: _____

ISBN (Optional Choice)

      Kindle ISBN _____

      Your ISBN _____

      Publisher (optional) _____

**Kindle eBook Pricing**

KDP Select Enrollment (Optional)   Yes ___     No ___

Territories (check one)

     ___ All territories

     ___ Individual territories (Note all your choices below)

     _____

     _____

     _____

     _____

     _____

     _____

     _____

     _____

**Book Title** _____

Royalty & Pricing - Select a royalty plan and set your Kindle eBook list prices below.

_____ 30%          _____ 70%

Your book file size after conversion is _____

Primary Marketplace _____

List Price Chosen _____      Currency _____

Rate _____      Delivery _____      Royalty _____


* Other Marketplace _____

List Price Chosen _____      Currency _____

Rate _____      Delivery _____      Royalty _____


* Other Marketplace _____

List Price Chosen _____      Currency _____

Rate _____      Delivery _____      Royalty _____


* Other Marketplace _____

List Price Chosen _____      Currency _____

Rate _____      Delivery _____      Royalty _____


* Other Marketplace _____

List Price Chosen _____      Currency _____

Rate _____      Delivery _____      Royalty _____


* Other Marketplace _____

List Price Chosen _____      Currency _____

Rate _____      Delivery _____      Royalty _____

**Book Title** _____

* Other Marketplace _____

List Price Chosen _____ Currency _____

Rate _____ Delivery _____ Royalty _____

* Other Marketplace _____

List Price Chosen _____ Currency _____

Rate _____ Delivery _____ Royalty _____

* Other Marketplace _____

List Price Chosen _____ Currency _____

Rate _____ Delivery _____ Royalty _____

* Other Marketplace _____

List Price Chosen _____ Currency _____

Rate _____ Delivery _____ Royalty _____

* Other Marketplace _____

List Price Chosen _____ Currency _____

Rate _____ Delivery _____ Royalty _____

* Other Marketplace _____

List Price Chosen _____ Currency _____

Rate _____ Delivery _____ Royalty _____

* Other Marketplace _____

List Price Chosen _____ Currency _____

Rate _____ Delivery _____ Royalty _____

**Book Title** _____

Matchbook

_____ Enroll my book in Kindle Matchbook

Book Lending

_____ Allow Kindle Book Lending

Terms & Conditions _____ Read

Save as Draft Date _____

Clicked Publish Your Kindle eBook Date _____

Published Notice from KDP Date _____

## Note Date & Changes Made

_____

_____

_____

_____

_____

_____

_____

_____

_____

_____

_____

_____

_____

_____

_____

_____

_____

**Book Title** _____

## Note Date & Changes Made

_____

_____

_____

_____

_____

_____

_____

_____

_____

_____

_____

_____

_____

_____

_____

_____

_____

_____

_____

_____

_____

_____

_____

_____

_____

_____

# BOOK 13 - Date _____

## Kindle eBook Details

Language _____

Book Title _____

Subtitle _____

Series _____ # \_\_\_\_

Edition Number (optional) \_\_\_\_\_

Author _____

Contributors (opt) _____

_____

_____

_____

Description: _____

_____

_____

_____

_____

_____

_____

_____

_____

_____

_____

Publishing Rights (circle or underline one)

I own the copyright

This is a public domain work

**Book Title** _____

Keywords (seven words or phrases)

_____

_____

_____

_____

_____

_____

_____

Categories (two)

_____

_____

_____

_____

Age & Grade Range

Children's Book age range (optional)

    Minimum _____          Maximum _____

U.S. grade range

    Minimum _____          Maximum _____

Adult Content        No    Yes

## Kindle eBook Content

Manuscript

    Digital Rights Management (DRM)

    Enable DRM on this Kindle eBooks?

        Yes _____       No _____

**Book Title** _____

Recommended formats for Kindle eBooks:
.doc, .docx, HTML, MOBI, ePub, RTF, Plain Text, and KPF.

Upload eBook manuscript

File name _____

Uploaded        Date _____

Spell Check

    ("Ignore All" doesn't always work)

File Updated        Date _____

File Updated        Date _____

File Updated        Date _____

**Interior Formatter** _____

Contact Info: _____

Cost: _____

Kindle eBook Cover (check one)

    ___ Use Cover Creator to make your book cover

    ___ Upload a cover you already have (JPG/TIFF only)

Upload your cover file

File name _____

Uploaded        Date _____

Kindle eBook Preview via Online Previewer

    ___ Launch Previewer        Approved date: _____

Downloadable Preview Options

    ___ On your computer        ___ On your Kindle device

**Book Title** _____

    Cover Updated   Date _____

    Cover Updated   Date _____

    Cover Updated   Date _____

    **Cover Designer** _____

    Contact Info: _____

    Cost: _____

ISBN (Optional Choice)

    Kindle ISBN _____

    Your ISBN _____

    Publisher (optional) _____

**Kindle eBook Pricing**

KDP Select Enrollment (Optional)    Yes ___    No ___

Territories (check one)

    ___ All territories

    ___ Individual territories (Note all your choices below)

_____

_____

_____

_____

_____

_____

_____

_____

_____

**Book Title** _____

Royalty & Pricing - Select a royalty plan and set your Kindle eBook list prices below.

_____ 30%         _____ 70%

Your book file size after conversion is _____

Primary Marketplace _____

List Price Chosen _____     Currency _____

Rate _____   Delivery _____   Royalty _____


\* Other Marketplace _____

List Price Chosen _____     Currency _____

Rate _____   Delivery _____   Royalty _____


\* Other Marketplace _____

List Price Chosen _____     Currency _____

Rate _____   Delivery _____   Royalty _____


\* Other Marketplace _____

List Price Chosen _____     Currency _____

Rate _____   Delivery _____   Royalty _____


\* Other Marketplace _____

List Price Chosen _____     Currency _____

Rate _____   Delivery _____   Royalty _____


\* Other Marketplace _____

List Price Chosen _____     Currency _____

Rate _____   Delivery _____   Royalty _____

**Book Title** _____

* Other Marketplace _____

List Price Chosen _____ Currency _____

Rate _____ Delivery _____ Royalty _____


* Other Marketplace _____

List Price Chosen _____ Currency _____

Rate _____ Delivery _____ Royalty _____


* Other Marketplace _____

List Price Chosen _____ Currency _____

Rate _____ Delivery _____ Royalty _____


* Other Marketplace _____

List Price Chosen _____ Currency _____

Rate _____ Delivery _____ Royalty _____


* Other Marketplace _____

List Price Chosen _____ Currency _____

Rate _____ Delivery _____ Royalty _____


* Other Marketplace _____

List Price Chosen _____ Currency _____

Rate _____ Delivery _____ Royalty _____


* Other Marketplace _____

List Price Chosen _____ Currency _____

Rate _____ Delivery _____ Royalty _____

**Book Title** _____

Matchbook

___ Enroll my book in Kindle Matchbook

Book Lending

___ Allow Kindle Book Lending

Terms & Conditions ___ Read

Save as Draft Date _____

Clicked Publish Your Kindle eBook Date _____

Published Notice from KDP Date _____

## Note Date & Changes Made

_____

_____

_____

_____

_____

_____

_____

_____

_____

_____

_____

_____

_____

_____

_____

**Book Title** _____

## Note Date & Changes Made

_____

_____

_____

_____

_____

_____

_____

_____

_____

_____

_____

_____

_____

_____

_____

_____

_____

_____

_____

_____

_____

# BOOK 14 - Date _____

## Kindle eBook Details

Language _____

Book Title _____

Subtitle _____

Series _____ # ____

Edition Number (optional) _____

Author _____

Contributors (opt) _____

_____

_____

Description: _____

_____

_____

_____

_____

_____

_____

_____

_____

_____

_____

_____

_____

Publishing Rights (circle or underline one)

I own the copyright

This is a public domain work

**Book Title** _____

Keywords (seven words or phrases)

_____

_____

_____

_____

_____

_____

_____

Categories (two)

_____

_____

_____

_____

Age & Grade Range

Children's Book age range (optional)

  Minimum ____      Maximum ____

U.S. grade range

  Minimum ____      Maximum ____

Adult Content     No   Yes

## Kindle eBook Content

Manuscript

 Digital Rights Management (DRM)

 Enable DRM on this Kindle eBooks?

  Yes ____    No ____

**Book Title** _____


Recommended formats for Kindle eBooks:

.doc, .docx, HTML, MOBI, ePub, RTF, Plain Text, and KPF.


Upload eBook manuscript

File name _____

Uploaded          Date _____

Spell Check

   ("Ignore All" doesn't always work)


File Updated     Date _____

File Updated     Date _____

File Updated     Date _____

**Interior Formatter** _____

Contact Info: _____

Cost: _____


Kindle eBook Cover (check one)

   ___ Use Cover Creator to make your book cover

   ___ Upload a cover you already have (JPG/TIFF only)


Upload your cover file

File name _____

Uploaded          Date _____

Kindle eBook Preview via Online Previewer

   ___ Launch Previewer          Approved date: _____

Downloadable Preview Options

      ___ On your computer          ___ On your Kindle device

**Book Title** _____

    Cover Updated    Date _____

    Cover Updated    Date _____

    Cover Updated    Date _____

    **Cover Designer** _____

    Contact Info: _____

    Cost: _____

ISBN (Optional Choice)

    Kindle ISBN _____

    Your ISBN _____

    Publisher (optional) _____

## Kindle eBook Pricing

KDP Select Enrollment (Optional)    Yes ___    No ___

Territories (check one)

    ___ All territories

    ___ Individual territories (Note all your choices below)

_____

_____

_____

_____

_____

_____

_____

_____

**Book Title** _____

Royalty & Pricing - Select a royalty plan and set your Kindle eBook list prices below.

___ 30%        ___ 70%

Your book file size after conversion is _____

Primary Marketplace _____

List Price Chosen _____     Currency _____

Rate _____   Delivery _____     Royalty _____


\* Other Marketplace _____

List Price Chosen _____     Currency _____

Rate _____   Delivery _____     Royalty _____


\* Other Marketplace _____

List Price Chosen _____     Currency _____

Rate _____   Delivery _____     Royalty _____


\* Other Marketplace _____

List Price Chosen _____     Currency _____

Rate _____   Delivery _____     Royalty _____


\* Other Marketplace _____

List Price Chosen _____     Currency _____

Rate _____   Delivery _____     Royalty _____


\* Other Marketplace _____

List Price Chosen _____     Currency _____

Rate _____   Delivery _____     Royalty _____

**Book Title** _____

* Other Marketplace _____

List Price Chosen _____      Currency _____

Rate _____  Delivery _____  Royalty _____


* Other Marketplace _____

List Price Chosen _____      Currency _____

Rate _____  Delivery _____  Royalty _____


* Other Marketplace _____

List Price Chosen _____      Currency _____

Rate _____  Delivery _____  Royalty _____


* Other Marketplace _____

List Price Chosen _____      Currency _____

Rate _____  Delivery _____  Royalty _____


* Other Marketplace _____

List Price Chosen _____      Currency _____

Rate _____  Delivery _____  Royalty _____


* Other Marketplace _____

List Price Chosen _____      Currency _____

Rate _____  Delivery _____  Royalty _____


* Other Marketplace _____

List Price Chosen _____      Currency _____

Rate _____  Delivery _____  Royalty _____

**Book Title** _____

Matchbook

    ___ Enroll my book in Kindle Matchbook

Book Lending

    ___ Allow Kindle Book Lending

Terms & Conditions ___ Read

    Save as Draft Date _____

    Clicked Publish Your Kindle eBook Date _____

    Published Notice from KDP Date _____

## Note Date & Changes Made

_____

_____

_____

_____

_____

_____

_____

_____

_____

_____

_____

_____

_____

_____

_____

_____

_____

_____

**Book Title** _____

## Note Date & Changes Made

_____
_____
_____
_____
_____
_____
_____
_____
_____
_____
_____
_____
_____
_____
_____
_____
_____
_____
_____
_____
_____
_____
_____
_____
_____
_____
_____

# BOOK 15 - Date _____

## Kindle eBook Details

Language _____

Book Title _____

Subtitle _____

Series _____ # _____

Edition Number (optional) _____

Author _____

Contributors (opt) _____

_____

_____

_____

Description: _____

_____

_____

_____

_____

_____

_____

_____

_____

_____

_____

_____

Publishing Rights (circle or underline one)

I own the copyright

This is a public domain work

**Book Title** _____

Keywords (seven words or phrases)

_____

_____

_____

_____

_____

_____

_____

Categories (two)

_____

_____

_____

_____

Age & Grade Range

Children's Book age range (optional)

    Minimum _____           Maximum _____

U.S. grade range

    Minimum _____           Maximum _____

Adult Content         No    Yes

## Kindle eBook Content

Manuscript

    Digital Rights Management (DRM)

    Enable DRM on this Kindle eBooks?

        Yes _____      No _____

**Book Title** _____

Recommended formats for Kindle eBooks:
.doc, .docx, HTML, MOBI, ePub, RTF, Plain Text, and KPF.

Upload eBook manuscript
File name _____
Uploaded        Date _____
Spell Check
        ("Ignore All" doesn't always work)

File Updated        Date _____
File Updated        Date _____
File Updated        Date _____
**Interior Formatter** _____
Contact Info: _____
Cost: _____

Kindle eBook Cover (check one)
        ___ Use Cover Creator to make your book cover
        ___ Upload a cover you already have (JPG/TIFF only)

Upload your cover file
File name _____
Uploaded        Date _____
Kindle eBook Preview via Online Previewer
        ___ Launch Previewer        Approved date: _____
Downloadable Preview Options
        ___ On your computer        ___ On your Kindle device

**Book Title** _____

    Cover Updated   Date _____

    Cover Updated   Date _____

    Cover Updated   Date _____

    **Cover Designer** _____

    Contact Info: _____

    Cost: _____

ISBN (Optional Choice)

    Kindle ISBN _____

    Your ISBN _____

    Publisher (optional) _____

**Kindle eBook Pricing**

KDP Select Enrollment (Optional)   Yes ____     No ____

Territories (check one)

    ____ All territories

    ____ Individual territories (Note all your choices below)

_____

_____

_____

_____

_____

_____

_____

_____

**Book Title** _____

Royalty & Pricing - Select a royalty plan and set your Kindle eBook list prices below.

_____ 30%　　　　_____ 70%

Your book file size after conversion is _____

Primary Marketplace _____

List Price Chosen _____　　Currency _____

Rate _____　Delivery _____　Royalty _____


\* Other Marketplace _____

List Price Chosen _____　　Currency _____

Rate _____　Delivery _____　Royalty _____


\* Other Marketplace _____

List Price Chosen _____　　Currency _____

Rate _____　Delivery _____　Royalty _____


\* Other Marketplace _____

List Price Chosen _____　　Currency _____

Rate _____　Delivery _____　Royalty _____


\* Other Marketplace _____

List Price Chosen _____　　Currency _____

Rate _____　Delivery _____　Royalty _____


\* Other Marketplace _____

List Price Chosen _____　　Currency _____

Rate _____　Delivery _____　Royalty _____

**Book Title** _____

* Other Marketplace _____

List Price Chosen _____      Currency _____

Rate _____      Delivery _____      Royalty _____


* Other Marketplace _____

List Price Chosen _____      Currency _____

Rate _____      Delivery _____      Royalty _____


* Other Marketplace _____

List Price Chosen _____      Currency _____

Rate _____      Delivery _____      Royalty _____


* Other Marketplace _____

List Price Chosen _____      Currency _____

Rate _____      Delivery _____      Royalty _____


* Other Marketplace _____

List Price Chosen _____      Currency _____

Rate _____      Delivery _____      Royalty _____


* Other Marketplace _____

List Price Chosen _____      Currency _____

Rate _____      Delivery _____      Royalty _____


* Other Marketplace _____

List Price Chosen _____      Currency _____

Rate _____      Delivery _____      Royalty _____

**Book Title** _____

Matchbook

_____ Enroll my book in Kindle Matchbook

Book Lending

_____ Allow Kindle Book Lending

Terms & Conditions _____ Read

Save as Draft Date _____

Clicked Publish Your Kindle eBook Date _____

Published Notice from KDP Date _____

## Note Date & Changes Made

_____

_____

_____

_____

_____

_____

_____

_____

_____

_____

_____

_____

_____

_____

_____

_____

**Book Title** _____

## Note Date & Changes Made

_____

_____

_____

_____

_____

_____

_____

_____

_____

_____

_____

_____

_____

_____

_____

_____

_____

_____

_____

_____

_____

# BOOK 16 - Date _____

## Kindle eBook Details

Language _____

Book Title _____

Subtitle _____

Series _____ # \_\_\_\_

Edition Number (optional) \_\_\_\_\_

Author _____

Contributors (opt) _____

_____

_____

_____

Description: _____

_____

_____

_____

_____

_____

_____

_____

_____

_____

_____

Publishing Rights (circle or underline one)

I own the copyright

This is a public domain work

**Book Title** _____

Keywords (seven words or phrases)

_____

_____

_____

_____

_____

_____

_____

Categories (two)

_____

_____

_____

_____

Age & Grade Range

Children's Book age range (optional)

    Minimum _____        Maximum _____

U.S. grade range

    Minimum _____        Maximum _____

Adult Content        No    Yes

## Kindle eBook Content

Manuscript

    Digital Rights Management (DRM)

    Enable DRM on this Kindle eBooks?

        Yes _____      No _____

**Book Title** _____

Recommended formats for Kindle eBooks:

.doc, .docx, HTML, MOBI, ePub, RTF, Plain Text, and KPF.

Upload eBook manuscript

File name _____

Uploaded          Date _____

Spell Check

     ("Ignore All" doesn't always work)

File Updated     Date _____

File Updated     Date _____

File Updated     Date _____

**Interior Formatter** _____

Contact Info: _____

Cost: _____

Kindle eBook Cover (check one)

    ___ Use Cover Creator to make your book cover

    ___ Upload a cover you already have (JPG/TIFF only)

Upload your cover file

File name _____

Uploaded          Date _____

Kindle eBook Preview via Online Previewer

    ___ Launch Previewer          Approved date: _____

Downloadable Preview Options

    ___ On your computer          ___ On your Kindle device

**Book Title** _____

    Cover Updated   Date _____

    Cover Updated   Date _____

    Cover Updated   Date _____

    **Cover Designer** _____

    Contact Info: _____

    Cost: _____

ISBN (Optional Choice)

    Kindle ISBN _____

    Your ISBN _____

    Publisher (optional) _____

**Kindle eBook Pricing**

KDP Select Enrollment (Optional)   Yes ____    No ____

Territories (check one)

    ____ All territories

    ____ Individual territories (Note all your choices below)

_____

_____

_____

_____

_____

_____

_____

_____

_____

_____

**Book Title** _____

Royalty & Pricing - Select a royalty plan and set your Kindle eBook list prices below.

_____ 30%          _____ 70%

Your book file size after conversion is _____

Primary Marketplace _____

List Price Chosen _____          Currency _____

Rate _____     Delivery _____     Royalty _____

* Other Marketplace _____

List Price Chosen _____          Currency _____

Rate _____     Delivery _____     Royalty _____

* Other Marketplace _____

List Price Chosen _____          Currency _____

Rate _____     Delivery _____     Royalty _____

* Other Marketplace _____

List Price Chosen _____          Currency _____

Rate _____     Delivery _____     Royalty _____

* Other Marketplace _____

List Price Chosen _____          Currency _____

Rate _____     Delivery _____     Royalty _____

* Other Marketplace _____

List Price Chosen _____          Currency _____

Rate _____     Delivery _____     Royalty _____

**Book Title** _____

\* Other Marketplace _____

List Price Chosen _____ Currency _____

Rate _____ Delivery _____ Royalty _____


\* Other Marketplace _____

List Price Chosen _____ Currency _____

Rate _____ Delivery _____ Royalty _____


\* Other Marketplace _____

List Price Chosen _____ Currency _____

Rate _____ Delivery _____ Royalty _____


\* Other Marketplace _____

List Price Chosen _____ Currency _____

Rate _____ Delivery _____ Royalty _____


\* Other Marketplace _____

List Price Chosen _____ Currency _____

Rate _____ Delivery _____ Royalty _____


\* Other Marketplace _____

List Price Chosen _____ Currency _____

Rate _____ Delivery _____ Royalty _____


\* Other Marketplace _____

List Price Chosen _____ Currency _____

Rate _____ Delivery _____ Royalty _____

**Book Title** _____

Matchbook

    ___ Enroll my book in Kindle Matchbook

Book Lending

    ___ Allow Kindle Book Lending

Terms & Conditions ___ Read

    Save as Draft Date _____

    Clicked Publish Your Kindle eBook Date _____

    Published Notice from KDP Date _____

## Note Date & Changes Made

_____

_____

_____

_____

_____

_____

_____

_____

_____

_____

_____

_____

_____

_____

**Book Title** _____

## Note Date & Changes Made

_____

_____

_____

_____

_____

_____

_____

_____

_____

_____

_____

_____

_____

_____

_____

_____

_____

_____

_____

_____

_____

_____

_____

# BOOK 17 - Date _____

## Kindle eBook Details

Language _____

Book Title _____

Subtitle _____

Series _____ # _____

Edition Number (optional) _____

Author _____

Contributors (opt) _____

_____

_____

_____

Description: _____

_____

_____

_____

_____

_____

_____

_____

_____

_____

_____

Publishing Rights (circle or underline one)

      I own the copyright

      This is a public domain work

**Book Title** _____

Keywords (seven words or phrases)

_____

_____

_____

_____

_____

_____

_____

Categories (two)

_____

_____

_____

_____

Age & Grade Range

Children's Book age range (optional)

    Minimum _____          Maximum _____

U.S. grade range

    Minimum _____          Maximum _____

Adult Content          No     Yes

## Kindle eBook Content

Manuscript

    Digital Rights Management (DRM)

    Enable DRM on this Kindle eBooks?

        Yes _____      No _____

**Book Title** _____

Recommended formats for Kindle eBooks:

.doc, .docx, HTML, MOBI, ePub, RTF, Plain Text, and KPF.

Upload eBook manuscript

File name _____

Uploaded      Date _____

Spell Check

     ("Ignore All" doesn't always work)

File Updated    Date _____

File Updated    Date _____

File Updated    Date _____

**Interior Formatter** _____

Contact Info: _____

Cost: _____

Kindle eBook Cover (check one)

    ___ Use Cover Creator to make your book cover

    ___ Upload a cover you already have (JPG/TIFF only)

Upload your cover file

File name _____

Uploaded      Date _____

Kindle eBook Preview via Online Previewer

    ___ Launch Previewer    Approved date: _____

Downloadable Preview Options

    ___ On your computer    ___ On your Kindle device

**Book Title** _____

    Cover Updated   Date _____

    Cover Updated   Date _____

    Cover Updated   Date _____

    **Cover Designer** _____

    Contact Info: _____

    Cost: _____

ISBN (Optional Choice)

    Kindle ISBN _____

    Your ISBN _____

    Publisher (optional) _____

**Kindle eBook Pricing**

KDP Select Enrollment (Optional)   Yes ___    No ___

Territories (check one)

    ___ All territories

    ___ Individual territories (Note all your choices below)

_____

_____

_____

_____

_____

_____

_____

_____

_____

**Book Title** _____

Royalty & Pricing - Select a royalty plan and set your Kindle eBook list prices below.

_____ 30%          _____ 70%

Your book file size after conversion is _____

Primary Marketplace _____

List Price Chosen _____     Currency _____

Rate _____     Delivery _____     Royalty _____


* Other Marketplace _____

List Price Chosen _____     Currency _____

Rate _____     Delivery _____     Royalty _____


* Other Marketplace _____

List Price Chosen _____     Currency _____

Rate _____     Delivery _____     Royalty _____


* Other Marketplace _____

List Price Chosen _____     Currency _____

Rate _____     Delivery _____     Royalty _____


* Other Marketplace _____

List Price Chosen _____     Currency _____

Rate _____     Delivery _____     Royalty _____


* Other Marketplace _____

List Price Chosen _____     Currency _____

Rate _____     Delivery _____     Royalty _____

**Book Title** _____

* Other Marketplace _____

List Price Chosen _____    Currency _____

Rate _____    Delivery _____    Royalty _____


* Other Marketplace _____

List Price Chosen _____    Currency _____

Rate _____    Delivery _____    Royalty _____


* Other Marketplace _____

List Price Chosen _____    Currency _____

Rate _____    Delivery _____    Royalty _____


* Other Marketplace _____

List Price Chosen _____    Currency _____

Rate _____    Delivery _____    Royalty _____


* Other Marketplace _____

List Price Chosen _____    Currency _____

Rate _____    Delivery _____    Royalty _____


* Other Marketplace _____

List Price Chosen _____    Currency _____

Rate _____    Delivery _____    Royalty _____


* Other Marketplace _____

List Price Chosen _____    Currency _____

Rate _____    Delivery _____    Royalty _____

**Book Title** _____

Matchbook

    ___ Enroll my book in Kindle Matchbook

Book Lending

    ___ Allow Kindle Book Lending

Terms & Conditions ___ Read

    Save as Draft Date _____

    Clicked Publish Your Kindle eBook Date _____

    Published Notice from KDP Date _____

## Note Date & Changes Made

_____

_____

_____

_____

_____

_____

_____

_____

_____

_____

_____

_____

_____

_____

_____

_____

**Book Title** _____

## Note Date & Changes Made

_____

_____

_____

_____

_____

_____

_____

_____

_____

_____

_____

_____

_____

_____

_____

_____

_____

_____

_____

_____

_____

_____

# BOOK 18 - Date _____

## Kindle eBook Details

Language _____

Book Title _____

Subtitle _____

Series _____ # _____

Edition Number (optional) _____

Author _____

Contributors (opt) _____

_____

_____

_____

Description: _____

_____

_____

_____

_____

_____

_____

_____

_____

_____

_____

Publishing Rights (circle or underline one)

I own the copyright

This is a public domain work

**Book Title** _____

Keywords (seven words or phrases)

_____

_____

_____

_____

_____

_____

_____

Categories (two)

_____

_____

_____

_____

Age & Grade Range

Children's Book age range (optional)

    Minimum ____                 Maximum ____

U.S. grade range

    Minimum ____                 Maximum ____

Adult Content          No     Yes

## Kindle eBook Content

Manuscript

Digital Rights Management (DRM)

Enable DRM on this Kindle eBooks?

    Yes ____      No ____

**Book Title** _____

Recommended formats for Kindle eBooks:

.doc, .docx, HTML, MOBI, ePub, RTF, Plain Text, and KPF.


Upload eBook manuscript

File name _____

Uploaded          Date _____

Spell Check

      ("Ignore All" doesn't always work)


File Updated     Date _____

File Updated     Date _____

File Updated     Date _____

**Interior Formatter** _____

Contact Info: _____

Cost: _____


Kindle eBook Cover (check one)

    ____ Use Cover Creator to make your book cover

    ____ Upload a cover you already have (JPG/TIFF only)


Upload your cover file

File name _____

Uploaded          Date _____

Kindle eBook Preview via Online Previewer

    ____ Launch Previewer        Approved date: _____

Downloadable Preview Options

      ____ On your computer        ____ On your Kindle device

**Book Title** _____

    Cover Updated   Date _____

    Cover Updated   Date _____

    Cover Updated  Date _____

    **Cover Designer** _____

    Contact Info: _____

    Cost: _____

ISBN (Optional Choice)

    Kindle ISBN _____

    Your ISBN _____

    Publisher (optional) _____

## Kindle eBook Pricing

KDP Select Enrollment (Optional)   Yes ___     No ___

Territories (check one)

    ___ All territories

    ___ Individual territories (Note all your choices below)

_____

_____

_____

_____

_____

_____

_____

_____

_____

**Book Title** _____

Royalty & Pricing - Select a royalty plan and set your Kindle eBook list prices below.

_____ 30%        _____ 70%

Your book file size after conversion is _____

Primary Marketplace _____

List Price Chosen _____    Currency _____

Rate _____    Delivery _____    Royalty _____


\* Other Marketplace _____

List Price Chosen _____    Currency _____

Rate _____    Delivery _____    Royalty _____


\* Other Marketplace _____

List Price Chosen _____    Currency _____

Rate _____    Delivery _____    Royalty _____


\* Other Marketplace _____

List Price Chosen _____    Currency _____

Rate _____    Delivery _____    Royalty _____


\* Other Marketplace _____

List Price Chosen _____    Currency _____

Rate _____    Delivery _____    Royalty _____


\* Other Marketplace _____

List Price Chosen _____    Currency _____

Rate _____    Delivery _____    Royalty _____

**Book Title** _____

* Other Marketplace _____

List Price Chosen _____  Currency _____

Rate _____  Delivery _____  Royalty _____


* Other Marketplace _____

List Price Chosen _____  Currency _____

Rate _____  Delivery _____  Royalty _____


* Other Marketplace _____

List Price Chosen _____  Currency _____

Rate _____  Delivery _____  Royalty _____


* Other Marketplace _____

List Price Chosen _____  Currency _____

Rate _____  Delivery _____  Royalty _____


* Other Marketplace _____

List Price Chosen _____  Currency _____

Rate _____  Delivery _____  Royalty _____


* Other Marketplace _____

List Price Chosen _____  Currency _____

Rate _____  Delivery _____  Royalty _____


* Other Marketplace _____

List Price Chosen _____  Currency _____

Rate _____  Delivery _____  Royalty _____

**Book Title** _____

Matchbook

___ Enroll my book in Kindle Matchbook

Book Lending

___ Allow Kindle Book Lending

Terms & Conditions ___ Read

Save as Draft Date _____

Clicked Publish Your Kindle eBook Date _____

Published Notice from KDP Date _____

## Note Date & Changes Made

_____

_____

_____

_____

_____

_____

_____

_____

_____

_____

_____

_____

_____

_____

_____

_____

_____

**Book Title** _____

## Note Date & Changes Made

_____

_____

_____

_____

_____

_____

_____

_____

_____

_____

_____

_____

_____

_____

_____

_____

_____

_____

_____

_____

_____

_____

_____

# BOOK 19 - Date _____

## Kindle eBook Details

Language _____

Book Title _____

Subtitle _____

Series _____ # ____

Edition Number (optional) _____

Author _____

Contributors (opt) _____

_____

_____

_____

Description: _____

_____

_____

_____

_____

_____

_____

_____

_____

_____

_____

_____

Publishing Rights (circle or underline one)

      I own the copyright

      This is a public domain work

**Book Title** _____

Keywords (seven words or phrases)

_____

_____

_____

_____

_____

_____

_____

Categories (two)

_____

_____

_____

_____

Age & Grade Range

Children's Book age range (optional)

    Minimum _____          Maximum _____

U.S. grade range

    Minimum _____          Maximum _____

Adult Content        No    Yes

## Kindle eBook Content

Manuscript

    Digital Rights Management (DRM)

    Enable DRM on this Kindle eBooks?

        Yes _____        No _____

**Book Title** _____

Recommended formats for Kindle eBooks:
.doc, .docx, HTML, MOBI, ePub, RTF, Plain Text, and KPF.

Upload eBook manuscript
File name _____
Uploaded        Date _____
Spell Check
     ("Ignore All" doesn't always work)

File Updated    Date _____
File Updated    Date _____
File Updated    Date _____
**Interior Formatter** _____
Contact Info: _____
Cost: _____

Kindle eBook Cover (check one)
    ____ Use Cover Creator to make your book cover
    ____ Upload a cover you already have (JPG/TIFF only)

Upload your cover file
File name _____
Uploaded        Date _____
Kindle eBook Preview via Online Previewer
    ____ Launch Previewer        Approved date: _____
Downloadable Preview Options
    ____ On your computer        ____ On your Kindle device

**Book Title** _____

    Cover Updated    Date _____

    Cover Updated    Date _____

    Cover Updated    Date _____

    **Cover Designer** _____

    Contact Info: _____

    Cost: _____

ISBN (Optional Choice)

    Kindle ISBN _____

    Your ISBN _____

    Publisher (optional) _____

## Kindle eBook Pricing

KDP Select Enrollment (Optional)    Yes ____    No ____

Territories (check one)

    ____ All territories

    ____ Individual territories (Note all your choices below)

_____

_____

_____

_____

_____

_____

_____

_____

_____

**Book Title** _____

Royalty & Pricing - Select a royalty plan and set your Kindle eBook list prices below.

_____ 30%        _____ 70%

Your book file size after conversion is _____

Primary Marketplace _____

List Price Chosen _____        Currency _____

Rate _____        Delivery _____        Royalty _____


* Other Marketplace _____

List Price Chosen _____        Currency _____

Rate _____        Delivery _____        Royalty _____


* Other Marketplace _____

List Price Chosen _____        Currency _____

Rate _____        Delivery _____        Royalty _____


* Other Marketplace _____

List Price Chosen _____        Currency _____

Rate _____        Delivery _____        Royalty _____


* Other Marketplace _____

List Price Chosen _____        Currency _____

Rate _____        Delivery _____        Royalty _____


* Other Marketplace _____

List Price Chosen _____        Currency _____

Rate _____        Delivery _____        Royalty _____

**Book Title** _____

* Other Marketplace _____

List Price Chosen _____ Currency _____

Rate _____ Delivery _____ Royalty _____


* Other Marketplace _____

List Price Chosen _____ Currency _____

Rate _____ Delivery _____ Royalty _____


* Other Marketplace _____

List Price Chosen _____ Currency _____

Rate _____ Delivery _____ Royalty _____


* Other Marketplace _____

List Price Chosen _____ Currency _____

Rate _____ Delivery _____ Royalty _____


* Other Marketplace _____

List Price Chosen _____ Currency _____

Rate _____ Delivery _____ Royalty _____


* Other Marketplace _____

List Price Chosen _____ Currency _____

Rate _____ Delivery _____ Royalty _____


* Other Marketplace _____

List Price Chosen _____ Currency _____

Rate _____ Delivery _____ Royalty _____

**Book Title** _____

Matchbook

 ___ Enroll my book in Kindle Matchbook

Book Lending

 ___ Allow Kindle Book Lending

Terms & Conditions ___ Read

 Save as Draft Date _____

 Clicked Publish Your Kindle eBook Date _____

 Published Notice from KDP Date _____

## Note Date & Changes Made

_____

_____

_____

_____

_____

_____

_____

_____

_____

_____

_____

_____

_____

_____

_____

_____

_____

_____

_____

_____

**Book Title** _____

## Note Date & Changes Made

_____

_____

_____

_____

_____

_____

_____

_____

_____

_____

_____

_____

_____

_____

_____

_____

_____

_____

_____

_____

_____

_____

_____

_____

_____

# BOOK 20 - Date _____

## Kindle eBook Details

Language _____

Book Title _____

Subtitle _____

Series _____ # _____

Edition Number (optional) _____

Author _____

Contributors (opt) _____

_____

_____

_____

Description: _____

_____

_____

_____

_____

_____

_____

_____

_____

_____

_____

_____

Publishing Rights (circle or underline one)

       I own the copyright

       This is a public domain work

**Book Title** _____

Keywords (seven words or phrases)

_____

_____

_____

_____

_____

_____

_____

Categories (two)

_____

_____

_____

Age & Grade Range

Children's Book age range (optional)

    Minimum _____             Maximum _____

U.S. grade range

    Minimum _____             Maximum _____

Adult Content          No     Yes

## Kindle eBook Content

Manuscript

    Digital Rights Management (DRM)

    Enable DRM on this Kindle eBooks?

        Yes _____         No _____

**Book Title** _____

Recommended formats for Kindle eBooks:
.doc, .docx, HTML, MOBI, ePub, RTF, Plain Text, and KPF.

Upload eBook manuscript

File name _____

Uploaded        Date _____

Spell Check

    ("Ignore All" doesn't always work)

File Updated        Date _____

File Updated        Date _____

File Updated        Date _____

**Interior Formatter** _____

Contact Info: _____

Cost: _____

Kindle eBook Cover (check one)

    ___ Use Cover Creator to make your book cover

    ___ Upload a cover you already have (JPG/TIFF only)

Upload your cover file

File name _____

Uploaded        Date _____

Kindle eBook Preview via Online Previewer

    ___ Launch Previewer        Approved date: _____

Downloadable Preview Options

    ___ On your computer        ___ On your Kindle device

**Book Title** _____

    Cover Updated   Date _____

    Cover Updated   Date _____

    Cover Updated   Date _____

    **Cover Designer** _____

    Contact Info: _____

    Cost: _____

ISBN (Optional Choice)

    Kindle ISBN _____

    Your ISBN _____

    Publisher (optional) _____

**Kindle eBook Pricing**

KDP Select Enrollment (Optional)   Yes ___   No ___

Territories (check one)

    ___ All territories

    ___ Individual territories (Note all your choices below)

_____

_____

_____

_____

_____

_____

_____

_____

_____

**Book Title** _____

Royalty & Pricing - Select a royalty plan and set your Kindle eBook list prices below.

_____ 30%       _____ 70%

Your book file size after conversion is _____

Primary Marketplace _____

List Price Chosen _____     Currency _____

Rate _____   Delivery _____   Royalty _____


* Other Marketplace _____

List Price Chosen _____     Currency _____

Rate _____   Delivery _____   Royalty _____


* Other Marketplace _____

List Price Chosen _____     Currency _____

Rate _____   Delivery _____   Royalty _____


* Other Marketplace _____

List Price Chosen _____     Currency _____

Rate _____   Delivery _____   Royalty _____


* Other Marketplace _____

List Price Chosen _____     Currency _____

Rate _____   Delivery _____   Royalty _____


* Other Marketplace _____

List Price Chosen _____     Currency _____

Rate _____   Delivery _____   Royalty _____

**Book Title** _____

* Other Marketplace _____

List Price Chosen _____ Currency _____

Rate _____ Delivery _____ Royalty _____


* Other Marketplace _____

List Price Chosen _____ Currency _____

Rate _____ Delivery _____ Royalty _____


* Other Marketplace _____

List Price Chosen _____ Currency _____

Rate _____ Delivery _____ Royalty _____


* Other Marketplace _____

List Price Chosen _____ Currency _____

Rate _____ Delivery _____ Royalty _____


* Other Marketplace _____

List Price Chosen _____ Currency _____

Rate _____ Delivery _____ Royalty _____


* Other Marketplace _____

List Price Chosen _____ Currency _____

Rate _____ Delivery _____ Royalty _____


* Other Marketplace _____

List Price Chosen _____ Currency _____

Rate _____ Delivery _____ Royalty _____

**Book Title** _____

Matchbook

___ Enroll my book in Kindle Matchbook

Book Lending

___ Allow Kindle Book Lending

Terms & Conditions ___ Read

Save as Draft Date _____

Clicked Publish Your Kindle eBook Date _____

Published Notice from KDP Date _____

## Note Date & Changes Made

_____

_____

_____

_____

_____

_____

_____

_____

_____

_____

_____

_____

_____

_____

_____

_____

**Book Title** _____

## Note Date & Changes Made

_____

_____

_____

_____

_____

_____

_____

_____

_____

_____

_____

_____

_____

_____

_____

_____

_____

_____

_____

_____

_____

_____

_____

_____

_____

# About the Creator of
# WestWard Journals

Marsha Ward writes authentic historical fiction, and nonfiction having to do with writing. Her novels include The Owen Family Saga series, the Shenandoah Neighbors series, and many other works of fiction. Her nonfiction books include *The Checklist: Indie Publishing My Way*, *Rapid Recipes for Writers . . . And Other Busy People*, and *From Julia's Kitchen: Owen Family Cookery*.

Find her online at Amazon or at marshaward.com.

www.ingramcontent.com/pod-product-compliance
Lightning Source LLC
Chambersburg PA
CBHW050126280326

41933CB00010B/1265